THE STORY OF THE DALLAS MAVERICKS

Derek Harper

Jalen Brunson

A HISTORY OF HOOPS

THE STORY OF THE

DALLAS
MAVERICKS

JIM WHITING

Wesley Matthews

CREATIVE EDUCATION / CREATIVE PAPERBACKS

Published by Creative Education and Creative Paperbacks
P.O. Box 227, Mankato, Minnesota 56002
Creative Education and Creative Paperbacks are imprints of
The Creative Company
www.thecreativecompany.us

Design and production by Blue Design (www.bluedes.com)
Art direction by Rita Marshall
Production layout by Rachel Klimpel and Ciara Beitlich

Photographs by AP Images (Tony Gutierrez), Getty (Jonathan Bachman,
Bill Baptist, Andrew D. Bernstein, Paul Buck, Kevork Djansezian, Stephen
Dunn, Focus On Sport, Glenn James, Jacob Kupferman, Andy Lyons, Ronald
Martinez, Layne Murdoch, Mike Powell, Andreas Rentz, John F. Rhodes,
Joe Robbins, Bob Rosato, Matt Rourke), Newscom (Jose Luis Villegas/ZUMA
Press), SBNation (Jason Kidd), Shutterstock (Brocreative, Andrey Burmakin,
Valentin Valkov)

Library of Congress Cataloging-in-Publication Data
Names: Whiting, Jim, 1943- author.
Title: The story of the Dallas Mavericks / by Jim Whiting.
Description: Mankato, Minnesota : Creative Education | Creative
    Paperbacks, [2023] | Series: Creative Sports: A History of Hoops | Includes
    index. | Audience: Ages 8-12 | Audience: Grades 4-6 | Summary: "Middle
    grade basketball fans are introduced to the extraordinary history
    of NBA's Dallas Mavs with a photo-laden narrative of their greatest
    successes and losses"-- Provided by publisher.
Identifiers: LCCN 2022007525 (print) | LCCN 2022007526 (ebook) | ISBN
    9781640266230 (library binding) | ISBN 9781682771792 (paperback) | ISBN
    9781640007642 (ebook)
Subjects: LCSH: Dallas Mavericks (Basketball team)--History--Juvenile
    literature.
Classification: LCC GV885.52.D34 W453 2023 (print) | LCC GV885.52.D34
    (ebook) | DDC 796.323/64097642812--dc23/eng/20220520
LC record available at https://lccn.loc.gov/2022007525
LC ebook record available at https://lccn.loc.gov/2022007526

Steve Nash

CONTENTS

LEGENDS OF THE HARDWOOD

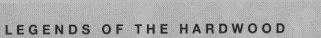

Jason Terry

WELL WORTH THE WAIT

Not many people thought the Dallas Mavericks had a chance in the 2010–11 National Basketball Association (NBA) Finals. Their opponent, the Miami Heat, boasted three of the league's superstars: LeBron James, Chris Bosh, and Dwayne Wade. The series turned out to be much closer than expected. The teams split the first four games. All but one was decided by three points or less.

In the crucial Game 5, Miami led by four points with less than five minutes left. Before the game, Linda Jo Carter—the wife of original owner Don Carter—pulled point/shooting guard Jason Terry aside. He had a reputation for having a big mouth. Sometimes his words were better than his shooting. "You talked it up," she said. "And you better do it." Terry did do it. He sank a three-pointer with 3:23 to go. It tied the score. Less than a minute later, Terry fed the ball to power forward/center Dirk Nowitzki for a thunderous dunk. The Mavs were up by two. Then Terry passed to fellow guard Jason Kidd for a three-pointer. With a half minute left on the clock, Terry capped his run of brilliance with yet another three-point shot. That iced the game. Dallas went on to win, 112–103.

The Mavs won Game 6 as well. In the first half of the game, the Mavs were up by two. They slowly pulled away in the third quarter. Terry's 19-foot jump shot with less than two minutes remaining sealed the deal. The final score was 105–95. The Mavericks had their first NBA title! It capped a 30-year wait. "This is a true team," said coach Rick Carlisle. "We don't run fast or jump high. [But] these guys had each other's backs. We played the right way. . . . This is a phenomenal thing for the city of Dallas."

MOVING ON UP WITH THE MAVS

The Mavs history starts in 1980. A Buffalo Braves executive convinced several Dallas businessmen to form an expansion team. They began playing in the 1980–81 season. A Dallas radio station conducted a name-the-team contest. The name Mavericks won. It was a good fit with the cowboy heritage of Texas. It was also the name of a popular 1957–62 TV series. Actor James Garner was a part-owner of the team. In the Mavericks' first game, they faced their fellow Texas franchise, the San Antonio Spurs. They won 103–92. But wins were rare after that. Dallas stumbled to a 15–67 record. It was the worst in the NBA.

Their poor record had a silver lining. The Mavs received the top pick in the 1981 NBA Draft. They chose Mark Aguirre, a small forward and 1980 College Player of the Year. He averaged nearly 19 points as a rookie. They also added shooting guard Rolando Blackman. The two helped Dallas win 28 games in 1981–82. The team improved to 38 wins the following season. Things were starting to look up in the "Big D."

The Mavs roped in point/shooting guard Derek Harper in 1983. The team's young talent produced 43 wins. It was the Mavs' first winning record. Aguirre scored 2,330 points. That remains the team's single-season record. They made the playoffs. Dallas defeated the Seattle SuperSonics in the first round. They fell to the Los Angeles Lakers in the conference semifinals.

Mark Aguirre

The Mavs did well again in the 1984 NBA Draft. They added long-armed forward/center Sam Perkins. Dallas won 44 games that season but couldn't get beyond the first round of the playoffs. The Mavs traded for James Donaldson, a massive 7-foot-2 center. He provided size and strength under the basket. Dallas won 44 games again in 1985–86. The Mavs advanced to the conference semifinals before losing.

Everything seemed to come together in the 1986–87 season. Dallas drafted 6-foot-11 forward/center Roy Tarpley. "With Roy on the floor, we talk NBA championship," said Blackman. "He brings us that little piece of magic . . . you see in a player who is superior to everyone he plays against." Fans hoped Blackman was right. The Mavs piled up 55 wins that season. Perhaps the Mavs could win the NBA championship. They took the first step with a 151–129 blowout of the SuperSonics in the first game of the playoffs. But Seattle came back to take the next three games. Dallas's season was over. So was Dick Motta's time as the coach. He had led the team from the beginning.

Motta's replacement, John MacLeod, steered the team to 53 wins in 1987–88. Dallas beat the Houston Rockets in the first round of the playoffs. It knocked off the Denver Nuggets in the second round. The Mavs faced the Lakers in the conference finals. The Lakers had a better record and home-court advantage. That proved to be crucial. In Game 7 in Los Angeles, Dallas trailed by just a point at halftime. The Lakers dominated the second half. They won 117–102.

Mavs fans had high hopes for the next season. But Dallas suffered several setbacks. Tarpley was suspended. Aguirre demanded a trade. Donaldson was hurt. The Mavs stumbled to 38–44 and missed the playoffs. They rebounded in 1989–90 to win 47 games. But the Portland Trail Blazers swept them in the first round of the playoffs.

ROLANDO BLACKMAN
SHOOTING GUARD
HEIGHT: 6-FOOT-6
MAVERICKS SEASONS: 1981–92

RO-LLING ALONG

Rolando "Ro" Blackman was born in Panama City, Panama. His family moved to Brooklyn, New York when he was eight. He was a star at Kansas State University. In 1981, he joined the Mavs. He played in four All-Star Games with Dallas. He left as the team's all-time leading scorer with 16,643 points. That record lasted for 18 years until Dirk Nowitzki surpassed it. But Blackman had another distinction. He played in 865 games with Dallas and never fouled out. The team retired his jersey number 22 in 2000. He was the first Latino player in NBA history with that honor.

DALLAS MAVERICKS

Brad Davis

DALLAS VS. SEATTLE
NBA PLAYOFFS, FIRST ROUND
GAME 5
APRIL 26, 1984

MAVS MADNESS

No one expected the Mavericks to get into the playoffs in 1984. As such, their usual home court was booked for a tennis match. With just 36 hours notice, the team had to prepare another venue. Duct tape marked the three-point line. There were no 24-second shot clocks or instant replay. The game went into overtime. The Mavs led 105–102 with five seconds left. Seattle scored on a tip-in with a second left and tried to sink a Hail Mary at the last second. It wasn't close. The happy Mavs ran into their locker room to celebrate. However, the referees ordered a replay of that final second. The grumpy Mavericks put on their sweat-soaked uniforms and returned. Luckily, Seattle couldn't get off a shot. Mavs won! Sportswriter Richie Whitt called it "the craziest night in Dallas Mavericks history."

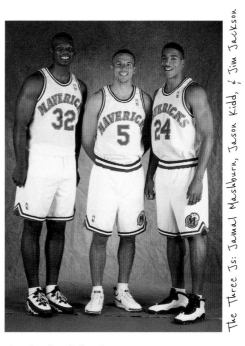

DARK DAYS IN DALLAS

T he 1989-90 season was the high-water mark for nearly a decade. Dallas slid to 28 wins in 1990–91 and 22 in the following season. Then the bottom fell out. The Mavericks scraped by with 11 wins in 1992–93. It was one of the worst seasons by any team in NBA history. They were almost as bad in 1993–94, winning just 13. These poor showings enabled Dallas to have some of the top picks in the NBA Draft. The team chose shooting guard/small forward Jim Jackson in 1992, small forward Jamal Mashburn in 1993, and Jason Kidd in 1994. They became known as the "Three J's." The Mavs won 36 games in 1994–95. Kidd became the first Maverick player selected as NBA Rookie of the Year. He shared the honor with Grant Hill of the Detroit Pistons. The next year, Kidd started in the All-Star Game.

Unfortunately, the reign of the Three Js was short-lived. Mashburn suffered a serious knee injury in 1995. Kidd and Jackson were traded. The Mavericks won just 24 games in 1996–97. They went through 27 players. Dallas added 7-foot-6 center Shawn Bradley and shooting guard/small forward Michael Finley before the 1997–98 season. Finley led his new team in scoring, assists, and steals. But the Mavs dropped to just 20 wins.

SHAWN BRADLEY
CENTER
HEIGHT: 7-FOOT-6
MAVERICKS SEASONS:
1997–2005

Shawn Bradley

A TALL TALE

Shawn Bradley came by his height naturally. His father was 6-foot-8 and his mother was an even 6 feet. Bradley matched his father's height while he was still in middle school. He was a versatile athlete who ran track and played baseball. The Philadelphia 76ers made him the second overall pick in the 1993 NBA Draft. He struggled in his first four years in the NBA. Coming to Dallas in a mid-season trade in the 1996–97 season helped revive his career. He averaged nearly 15 points and 9 rebounds a game in that season. Bradley was especially valuable on defense. His height made him an excellent shot blocker. His career average of 2.5 blocks per game ranks ninth in league history. Sadly, he suffered a bicycle accident in 2021 which paralyzed him.

Dirk Nowitzki

Dallas hit pay dirt in the 1998 NBA Draft. The team made a trade with the Milwaukee Bucks to select the German-born Dirk Nowitzki. He was somewhat of an international man of mystery. "Not a lot was known about the German game at that time," said Milwaukee general manager Larry Harris. Dallas coach Don Nelson knew better. "When I saw Dirk for the first time, he was the greatest 17- or 18-year-old or whatever he was that I'd ever witnessed," he said. (Nowitzki actually turned 20 five days before the draft.) The team also traded for point guard Steve Nash. Basketball author Chris Ballard called it "the greatest set of draft-day trades in NBA history . . . . That's two MVPs [Most Valuable Players] for two bench players."

Nowitzki wasn't an immediate sensation. He averaged only eight points a game in the lockout-shortened 1998–99 season. The Mavs finished just 19–31. Dallas did much better the following year. The team won 30 of its last 48 games, ending 40–42. Nowitzki averaged nearly 18 points a game. By this time, most of the parts for success were in place. Dallas just needed a spark to set them off.

MARK BUYS THE MAVS

n 2000, tech billionaire Mark Cuban bought the team. The coaching staff feared the worst. "Dirk [Nowitzki] hadn't kicked in, [Steve] Nash couldn't make a jump shot, so we literally went out and thought we were going to be fired the next day when we showed up," said assistant coach Donnie Nelson. His father, Don "Nellie" Nelson, was the team's head coach. New owners often release the current coaching and front office staffs. "Then the next day Mark walks in Nellie's office in a t-shirt, jeans, and his patented tennis shoes. And Nellie leans over to me and he goes, 'Son, I think we might have a chance with this one.'"

Cuban made it clear that he wouldn't accept mediocrity. He showed his willingness to pay top dollar for players. He also treated his players much better than they had been accustomed to. "He bought us a new plane, he got us a new arena, we started staying in nice hotels, we started to have food after games and after practices, and he just put Dallas basketball back on the map," Nowitzki said.

Those efforts paid off. Nash directed the offense. All-Star forward Juwan Howard joined Nowitzki and Finley to provide a scoring punch. The high-powered Mavs went 53–29 in 2000–01. It was their first winning record in a decade. Dallas lost in the conference semifinals that year and the next. The team soon became a melting pot of players from other countries. Nowitzki was German. Nash was from Canada. Three other players were foreign: center Wang Zhizhi (China), forward Eduardo Najera (Mexico), and guard Tariq Abdul-Wahad (France). "Having players that are national heroes adds quite a bit to the team," Cuban said.

MARK CUBAN
OWNER
MAVERICKS SEASONS:
2000–PRESENT

PUTTING THE MAVS ON THE MAP

Many people credit Mark Cuban with the rise of the Mavericks in
the 21st century. "Nobody was paying attention to the Mavericks
really and then Mark took over," said Dirk Nowitzki. Cuban likes
to wear a Mavs jersey at games and sit next to fans. He is one
of several investors on the TV series *Shark Tank*. They consider
investing in products that inventors present to them. Cuban likes
doing offbeat things. He served as a celebrity bartender. He worked
the counter at a Dairy Queen. He played basketball with the Harlem
Globetrotters. He even played Nowitzki in a game of one-on-one.
Nowitzki dunked on him and won.

DALLAS MAVERICKS

Dallas surged to 60 wins in 2002–03. In the conference finals, the Spurs defeated the Mavericks. "It was a matter of them turning their gear up a level, and we couldn't get any higher," explained Nelson. "That was the end of it." But it was hardly the end of Dallas's success. The Mavericks won "only" 52 games in 2003–04 but lost in the first round of the playoffs.

Dallas upped the victory total to 58 in 2004–05. Nelson stunned the team by stepping down late in the season. Assistant coach Avery Johnson replaced him. "I see a little slippage as a team," Nelson said. "The team is just responding better to Avery at this point." Dallas powered back to 60 wins the following season. Jason Terry was one key. He averaged 17 points a game. The Mavs charged through the first three rounds of the playoffs. They met the Heat in the NBA Finals. Dallas felt good about its chances. It had defeated the Heat in both regular-season games. The Mavs beat the Heat in the first two games. But Miami won the next four. Three of Dallas's losses were by three points or fewer.

Don Nelson

Avery Johnson

Josh Howard

DALLAS TAKES THE TITLE

The near miss made Dallas fans eagerly anticipate the following season. The Mavs didn't disappoint. They surged to 67 wins. It was a tie for the sixth-best record in NBA history at the time. Nowitzki had become one of the NBA's best big men. He consistently averaged 25 points and nearly 10 rebounds. The Mavs faced the Golden State Warriors in the playoffs. The Warriors snuck into the playoffs with a 42–40 record. Yet they became the first eighth seed to knock off the top seed in a best-of-seven series. One reason for the shocking upset may have been Nelson. He had become the Warriors' coach. "If there was one guy who knew how to defend Dirk [Nowitzki], it was the guy coaching the other team," Cuban said.

Dallas won at least 50 games in the next three seasons. But they suffered early playoff defeats. Before the 2010–11 season, Dallas added 7-foot-1 center Tyson Chandler. He was named to the NBA All-Defensive Team. Dallas won 57 games. Fans were encouraged when the Mavs beat Portland, 4 games to 2, in the first round. Nearly everyone wore "The Time Is Now" t-shirts to games. Dallas swept the Lakers in the second round. The Mavs silenced the Oklahoma City Thunder in the conference finals, 4 games to 1.

They faced Miami in the Finals. Most people thought that the Heat would easily win. Hardly anyone gave Dallas a chance. So the Mavericks played with chips on their shoulders. After losing the first game, they channeled that energy into winning four of the next five and become champions.

Tyson Chandler

**DALLAS VS. MIAMI
NBA FINALS
MAY 31–JUNE 12, 2011**

EARNING RESPECT

Most of the media attention before the 2010–11 Finals focused on Miami's "Big Three" of LeBron James, Chris Bosh, and Dwyane Wade. That didn't sit well with the Mavericks. For one thing, their seasons were virtually identical. Miami won 58 games. Dallas won 57. For another, the Mavericks had their own set of stars, such as Dirk Nowitzki and Jason Kidd. "We were being disrespected," said power/small forward Corey Brewer. "Nobody even talked about us. If you're going to disrespect us, we're going to show you that we're not to be disrespected." There was another factor. Before Game 4, Nowitzki was sick with a temperature of 102° F. He played anyway. James and Wade of the Heat openly mocked him. That upset the Mavs. "If you make fun of the big guy, you're making fun of everybody," said Brewer. It may have even been the turning point in the series. "It [the momentum] immediately just shifted," said small forward Caron Butler. "I'm telling you—I say this with the utmost confidence, I knew that we [were] going to have a [victory] parade in Dallas."

DALLAS MAVERICKS

LEGENDS
OF THE HARDWOOD

LUKA DONČIĆ
POINT GUARD/SHOOTING GUARD
HEIGHT: 6-FOOT-7
MAVERICKS SEASONS:
2018–PRESENT

LUKA CLAUS

With the COVID-19 pandemic raging during Christmas in 2021, Luka Dončić wanted to help young kids in his native country, Slovenia. He shipped gifts to patients in a children's hospital—LEGO sets, dollhouses, stuffed animals, Michael Jordan sportswear, and much more. Older kids got high-tech headphones. "These children are going through so much," he said. "I just hope this gives them a little bit of happiness during these difficult times." According to 12-year-old patient Hana, Dončić succeeded. "Since the pandemic, we don't get to have as many visitors or daily activities to pass the time," she said. "So when we're surprised with gifts from a global star like Luka, it's a good day!"

After taking the title, Dallas fans hoped for a repeat championship. But disagreements about money between the players and owners delayed the start of the 2011–12 season before they were resolved. Dallas went 36–30. The Thunder blew the Mavs out in the first round of the playoffs. With 41 wins the following season, the Mavericks missed the playoffs for the first time in 13 seasons. Dallas returned to the playoffs in the next three seasons. Each time the Mavs lost in the first round.

They fell on hard times during the next three seasons, finishing well out of playoff contention. There was one bright spot. On a draft-day trade with Atlanta, the Mavericks acquired Slovenian teenage sensation Luka Dončić in 2018. He averaged more than 21 points a game while pulling down nearly 8 rebounds and dishing out more than 8 assists. He was an easy choice for NBA Rookie of the Year.

Nowitzki retired at the end of the 2018–19 season. In an era of free agency with players constantly switching teams, Nowitzki stood out. He played his entire NBA career in Dallas. He is the team's all-time leading scorer. His 31,560 points are nearly double the next highest; Blackman had 16,643. He is also the NBA's career leader in three-point shots among players who are seven feet or taller.

In the 2019–2020 season, Dončić had an even better season, averaging nearly 29 points and 9 assists. He was a starter in the All-Star Game. The Mavericks had the distinction of playing the last game before the COVID-19 pandemic suspended the season for nearly four months. When play resumed in late July, the Mavs became the seventh seed in the Western Conference. They faced the Los Angeles Clippers. Dončić provided the highlight for Dallas. His buzzer-beating three-pointer in Game 4 tied the series. He became the youngest-ever player to hit one in the playoffs. But the Clippers won the next two to take the series. There was one consolation. Dončić was named to the All-NBA First Team. He repeated that honor in 2020–21. But once again Dallas couldn't get by the Clippers in the first round.

Dallas finished 52–30 in the following season. Point guard Jalen Brunson averaged more than 16 points per game. Veteran shooting/point guard Spencer Dinwiddie added another 15. Dallas defeated Utah in the first round of the playoffs, 4 games to 2. In the conference semifinals, they took the Phoenix Suns, who had the league's best record, to a deciding Game 7. Playing in Phoenix, the Mavs embarrassed the Suns with a 123–90 blowout. But they lost to the Warriors in the Western Conference finals, 4 games to 1. Dallas added a key player in the 2022-23 season. The team acquired Christian Wood in a trade from Houston. The forward/center averaged over 19 points and nearly 10 rebounds a game for the Rockets in two prior seasons.

The Mavericks have been one of the NBA's most consistent teams since the turn of the century. Fans feel confident that their team will always be in the playoffs. They hope that another championship banner will soon be raised in American Airlines Center.

Dwight Powell